After-School FUN

Karate

by JoAnn Early Macken

Reading consultant: Susan Nations, M.Ed., author/literacy coach/consultant

Please visit our web site at: www.earlyliteracy.cc
For a free color catalog describing Weekly Reader® Early Learning Library's list
of high-quality books, call 1-877-445-5824 (USA) or 1-800-387-3178 (Canada).
Weekly Reader® Early Learning Library's fax: (414) 336-0164.

Library of Congress Cataloging-in-Publication Data

Macken, JoAnn Early, 1953-
    Karate / by JoAnn Early Macken.
        p. cm. — (After-school fun)
    Includes bibliographical references and index.
    ISBN 0-8368-4514-5 (lib. bdg.)
    ISBN 0-8368-4521-8 (softcover)
    1. Karate—Juvenile literature. I. Title.
GV1114.3.M33   2005
796.815'3—dc22   2004043123

This edition first published in 2005 by
Weekly Reader® Early Learning Library
330 West Olive Street, Suite 100
Milwaukee, WI 53212 USA

Photographer: Gregg Andersen
Picture research: Diane Laska-Swanke
Art direction and page layout: Tammy West

Printed in the United States of America

1 2 3 4 5 6 7 8 9 09 08 07 06 05

Note to Educators and Parents

Reading is such an exciting adventure for young children!
They are beginning to integrate their oral language skills with
written language. To encourage children along the path to
early literacy, books must be colorful, engaging, and interesting;
they should invite the young reader to explore both the print
and the pictures.

After-School Fun is a new series designed to help children
read about the kinds of activities they enjoy in their free time.
In each book, young readers learn about a different artistic
endeavor, physical activity, or learning experience.

Each book is specially designed to support the young
reader in the reading process. The familiar topics are appealing
to young children and invite them to read — and reread —
again and again. The full-color photographs and enhanced
text further support the student during the reading process.

In addition to serving as wonderful picture books in schools,
libraries, homes, and other places where children learn to love
reading, these books are specifically intended to be read within
an instructional guided reading group. This small group setting
allows beginning readers to work with a fluent adult model as
they make meaning from the text. After children develop
fluency with the text and content, the book can be read
independently. Children and adults alike will find these books
supportive, engaging, and fun!

— Susan Nations, M.Ed., author, literacy coach,
and consultant in literacy development

After school, I go to karate class. I wear a white uniform called a *gi*. My belt, or *obi*, is white, too.

The teacher, or *sensei,* wears a black obi.
I bow to the sensei.
Bowing shows respect.

We start the class by stretching. We stretch our bodies. We stretch our legs.

We practice a **stance**, or position. This stance is called the straddle stance.

We practice a punch. This punch is called a lunge punch.

I practice a kick. This kick is called a side kick.

We learn how to block. A block stops a kick or a punch. Karate is meant for self-defense.

17

We learn a *kata*.
A **kata** is a pattern
of blocks, kicks, and
punches. A kata
looks like a dance.

In karate class, we learn control. We learn never to start fights. Karate helps us to be stronger and safer.

Glossary

block — to stop a movement

gi — a uniform worn for karate

kata — a pattern of blocks, kicks, and punches

obi — the belt that is worn with a gi

sensei — a teacher of martial arts, such as karate or judo

stance — a position

For More Information

Books

Chip and the Karate Kick. Anne Rockwell (HarperCollins)

Jojo's Flying Side Kick. Brian Pinkney (Simon & Schuster)

Karate Girl. Mary Leary (Farrar, Straus and Giroux)

Karate. Thomas Buckley (Child's World)

Web Sites

Edmonton Shotokan Karate School
www.karatedojo.com/
History, training, techniques, and more

Index

About the Author

JoAnn Early Macken is the author of two rhyming picture books, *Sing-Along Song* and *Cats on Judy*, and six other series of nonfiction books for beginning readers. Her poems have appeared in several children's magazines. A graduate of the M.F.A. in Writing for Children and Young Adults program at Vermont College, she lives in Wisconsin with her husband and their two sons. Visit her Web site at www.joannmacken.com.